Here is the top-notch Which Way crew that has volunteered to help you on your Tennessee travels:

I.Q. Sue is leading this adventure. She has big plans for sightseeing when the crew reaches Memphis.

Robomouse can't wait to roll past Fat Man's Squeeze at Rock City.

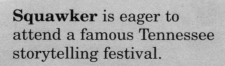

Squawker is eager to attend a famous Tennessee storytelling festival.

Table of Contents

WHO is heading for the WHICH WAY HALL OF FAME?

WHAT will be in the WHICH WAY MUSEUM?

WHERE will the WHICH WAY SUPERMAX MOVIE be filmed?

Memphis Meeting

You begin your journey in Memphis, the largest city in Tennessee. Memphis is famous for its music. It's known as both the "Home of the Blues" and the "Birthplace of Rock and Roll." But this Mississippi River city has many other things to offer, too. I.Q. Sue couldn't wait to start exploring the city. She arrived in town a day early and made a list of things for the crew to do.

The city map shows some popular Memphis destinations. Follow Sue's tour from one place to the next. At each location, you will find a code word. As you find each place, write its word on the correct line on the bottom of page 3.

Sue's List

1. Tour the Civil War headquarters of Ulysses S. Grant.

2. Let Willy record a souvenir tape at the studio B. B. King once used.

3. See the exhibits in a former motel.

4. Listen to a live performance of a blues band.

5. Take Squawker to see five feathered friends.

6. Walk the "entire length" of the Mississippi River.

7. See a famous Broadway show in downtown Memphis.

WROTE

SENATOR

ROOTS

THE

POLITICIAN

WHO

City Map Key

Peabody Hotel: Has a fountain in its lobby that is home to five mallard ducks

Orpheum Theatre: Place to see opera, ballet, and Broadway shows

Sun Studio: Recording studio where B. B. King and Elvis Presley launched their careers

The Pyramid: Contains an arena used for sports events and concerts

Beale Street Historic District: Street famous for blues music and a popular spot to hear live bands

Mud Island: Sights include a five-block-long scale model of the Mississippi River

Memphis Queen Riverboats: Paddleboats offering an old-time tour of the river

The National Civil Rights Museum: Exhibits housed in the Lorraine Motel, where Dr. Martin Luther King Jr. was assassinated

Hunt-Phelan Home: Historic mansion that was a Civil War headquarters for Ulysses S. Grant

CROSS

OUT

SUN

Did you visit all the sites and write the code words on these lines?

CROSS OUT THE PERSON WHO WROTE RODS

1   2   3   4   5   6   7

Now turn to page 28 and follow the instructions.

ERSON

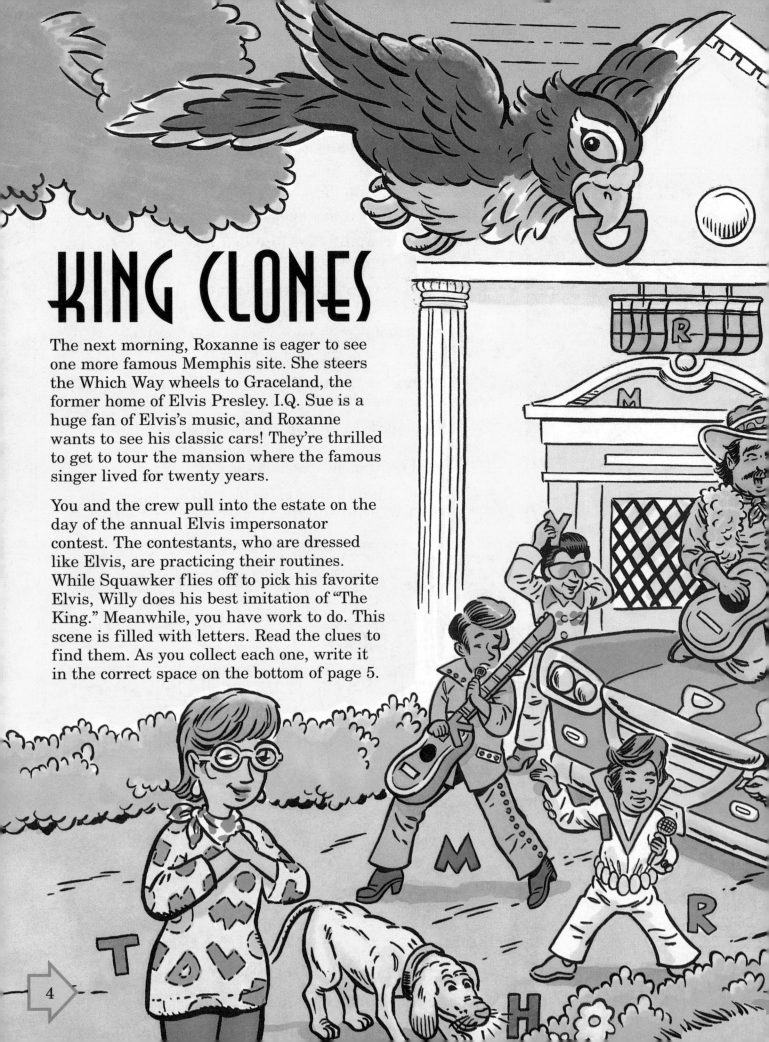

KING CLONES

The next morning, Roxanne is eager to see one more famous Memphis site. She steers the Which Way wheels to Graceland, the former home of Elvis Presley. I.Q. Sue is a huge fan of Elvis's music, and Roxanne wants to see his classic cars! They're thrilled to get to tour the mansion where the famous singer lived for twenty years.

You and the crew pull into the estate on the day of the annual Elvis impersonator contest. The contestants, who are dressed like Elvis, are practicing their routines. While Squawker flies off to pick his favorite Elvis, Willy does his best imitation of "The King." Meanwhile, you have work to do. This scene is filled with letters. Read the clues to find them. As you collect each one, write it in the correct space on the bottom of page 5.

4

1. The first letter is on the Which Way convertible.
2. The second letter is near the impersonator wearing blue suede shoes.
3. Squawker's got the third letter.
4. The fourth letter is being sniffed by a hound dog.
5. Look for the fifth letter on a white suit.
6. Robomouse found the sixth letter near some flowers.
7. One impersonator is using the seventh letter to play a guitar.
8. The eighth letter can be found on an animal statue.
9. The ninth letter is on the wrought iron balcony.
10. An impersonator is combing his hair with the last letter.

Have you filled in all the letters? Now follow the message:

Turn to page 28 and cross off

___ ___ ___ ___ ___ ___ ___ ___ ___ ___.
1   2   3   4   5   6   7   8   9   10

The Reel Deal

Willy has heard about a great fishing spot near some cypress trees on Reelfoot Lake. He decides to check it out. But first his stomach tells him to check out some local barbecue. He grabs some tasty pulled-pork sandwiches on the way out of Memphis and eats them on the bus ride north.

Willy reaches the lake just in time to rent a boat and get in a few casts before dark. Reelfoot is the largest natural lake in Tennessee and is home to more than fifty kinds of fish.

You can reel in some fish—and another clue—here. Circle the names of twenty types of fish in the grid on page 7. They are hidden forward, backward, up, down, and diagonally. When you have found them all, don't "de-bait." Row directly down to the bottom of the page.

REELFOOT FISH LIST

- Bass
- Bluegill
- Bowfin
- Bream
- Bullhead
- Chub
- Common carp
- Dace
- Drum
- Flier
- Gar
- Least madtom
- Minnow
- Mosquitofish
- Paddlefish
- Pickerel
- Shad
- Shiner
- Silverside
- White crappie

H P A D D L E F I S H T
H S S A B U L L H E A D
W H I T E C R A P P I E
L E L F W I D N N E C R
E O V F O A N R O A B E
R L E A S T M A D T O M
E S R L L I G E U L B
K H S P E F N U D A C R
C I I E L P N B Q R R E
I N D I I Z O E U S U A
P E E N I F W O B H O M
P R A C N O M M O C C M

Did you circle the names of all the fish?
Now write the leftover letters, in order from left to right
and top to bottom, in the spaces below:

THE WINNER OF
A NOBBLZPRACCO?
PRIBE

Use this clue to cross off a person on page 28.

HELLO, SHILOH

Meanwhile, the rest of the crew drives east to Shiloh National Military Park. This park was the scene of one of the fiercest battles of the Civil War. Thousands of Tennessee volunteers fought in the Civil War, as well as all previous U. S. wars. That's why the state is called the Volunteer State. Citizens of Tennessee had strong differences of opinion about the issues of the Civil War, including slavery. These differences divided towns—and even some families. Some men joined the Union Army, while others fought for the Confederacy.

Roxanne rents a bike and takes Robomouse on a tour of the battlefield. Squawker and Sue stay in the visitors' center to watch a film about the Battle of Shiloh. While they go to find seats, you have work to do. Circle the letter of the correct answer for each question about Tennessee. Then troop to the bottom of page 9.

1. Where do the Peabody Hotel ducks spend their nights?

e. Regal Roost   **i. Quack of Dawn Diner**
o. Royal Duck Palace

2. What highway connects the cities of Nashville and Memphis?

m. Route 64   **p. Interstate 40**
r. Natchez Trace Parkway

Don't Forget Your Map!
The answers to all the questions can be found somewhere on your Tennessee map.

3. What is the state flower of Tennessee?

c. tulip   **r. iris**
s. sunflower

4. In what year did Tennessee become the sixteenth state?

l. 1763 **t.** 1775 **y.** 1796

7. Who started a trading post where Nashville now stands?

a. Charles Charleville
e. Robert Robertson
s. Daniel Boone

5. What "first" was built on top of Lookout Mountain in the late 1920s?

a. high-powered telescope
s. miniature golf course
w. recording studio

8. How many states border Tennessee?

k. seven **r.** eight **y.** nine

Have you found the answers? Now write the letters you circled in the spaces below.

It is not the

o p r y s t a r
1 2 3 4 5 6 7 8

Use this information to cross off another person on page 28.

6. Which of these is *not* one of Tennessee's state songs?

d. "Rocky Top"
i. "When It's Iris Time in Tennessee"
t. "On Top of Ol' Smoky"

A Night at the Opry

The crew heads northeast on the scenic Natchez Trace Parkway. This is a winding road that follows a historic trail that was once used by Native Americans. Roxanne takes the parkway into Nashville, where you pick up Willy at the bus station.

Tennessee's capital city is also the nation's center of the country music industry. I.Q. Sue wants to see a country music show at the legendary Grand Ole Opry. Unfortunately, by the time Sue buys tickets, the show is nearly sold out. There aren't five seats left together, but at least everyone will get to see the show. Fiddle around with the clues to figure out where each crew member should sit. Then swing on down to the bottom of page 11.

CLUES:

1. Willy needs an aisle seat to stretch his legs.
2. Squawker and Sue have seats in the same row.
3. Robomouse will be the only Which Way crew member in his row.
4. Roxanne will be seated directly in front of Sue.

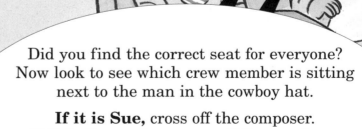

Did you find the correct seat for everyone?
Now look to see which crew member is sitting
next to the man in the cowboy hat.

If it is Sue, cross off the composer.
If it is Squawker, cross off the war hero.
If it is Roxanne, cross off the civil-rights worker.

Now turn to page 28 and use this clue to
cross off one final Tennessee citizen.

Parthenon Picnic

The next morning, the crew tours more of the Nashville area. Sue and Roxanne head outside of town to Hermitage, the former home of Andrew Jackson. "Old Hickory" was a hero of the War of 1812 and the seventh president of the United States. The others walk to the Country Music Hall of Fame and Museum. Willy likes the display of Gibson guitars, which are made in Nashville.

The group meets again in Nashville's Centennial Park. They gather by the Greek Parthenon, a life-sized copy of the famous temple in Greece. A day in "Music City USA" inspires Willy to pull out his old guitar. He plays as Squawker squawks along. While they sing a duet, you must work solo on this puzzle. Fill in the answers, then write the letters with numbers under them in the spaces at the top of page 13. Finally, tune into the clue at the bottom of the page.

1. The Ocoee River runs through a rocky gorge in this location.

Cherokee National Forest
　　1　　　　　　　　　　　　　2

2. The word *Chattanooga* has this meaning.

rock rising to a point
　　　　　　　3　　　4

3. This Tennessee city is the world capital of country music.

Nashville
5　6

4. Most of the area around Reelfoot Lake is considered this.

a nature preserve
7　8　　　　9

5. The Battle of Shiloh took place during this war.

The Civil War
　10　　11

6. About this many people visit the Great Smoky Mountains National Park each year.

nine million
　12　　　13

STATE MAP

Don't Forget Your Map!
Use the information on the *back* of your map to help you find the answers.

CROSS OFF EACH Y
11 1 4 6 6 4 2 2 9 7 11 10 8

IN THE LETTER CHART
12 5 3 10 9 13 9 3 3 9 1 11 10 7 1 3

Did you fill in all of the spaces above? Turn to page 29 and write the letter on the correct line and then follow the instructions.

Horsing Around

The crew leaves Nashville and drives south. The next stop is in Shelbyville. This town is the home of the Tennessee Walking Horse National Celebration. Each summer, this popular festival attracts thousands of people. The Tennessee walker is often called the "world's greatest show and pleasure horse." This gentle breed was originally developed near Shelbyville. Sue tells you that Tennessee is the only state to have a horse breed named for it.

An old friend of Willy's plans to enter a few horses in an upcoming competition. He invites Willy and the crew to watch the horses and riders practice. As they face the grandstand, your horse sense kicks in. You suspect there's a clue here. Use the letters you find to crack the code. Then trot to the bottom of page 15.

Have you cracked the code?
Now turn to page 29 and
follow the instructions.

Rocks and Rolls

You leave Shelbyville and go south and east to Chattanooga. Along the way, Sue reminds everyone to turn their watches ahead an hour. You have just driven into the Eastern Time Zone. Roxanne steers the Which Way wheels to nearby Rock City.

Rock City is a popular tourist attraction located on top of Chattanooga's Lookout Mountain. It is filled with natural rock formations. You decide to take a walk on the Enchanted Trail, where you stroll through tight places with names such as Fat Man's Squeeze. Robomouse thinks he sees a distant cousin and rolls off to say hello. The "cousin" turns out to be just a small mouse-shaped rock, but now Robomouse has strayed from the main trail. Help him find the path back to the group. Then find your way to the bottom of page 17.

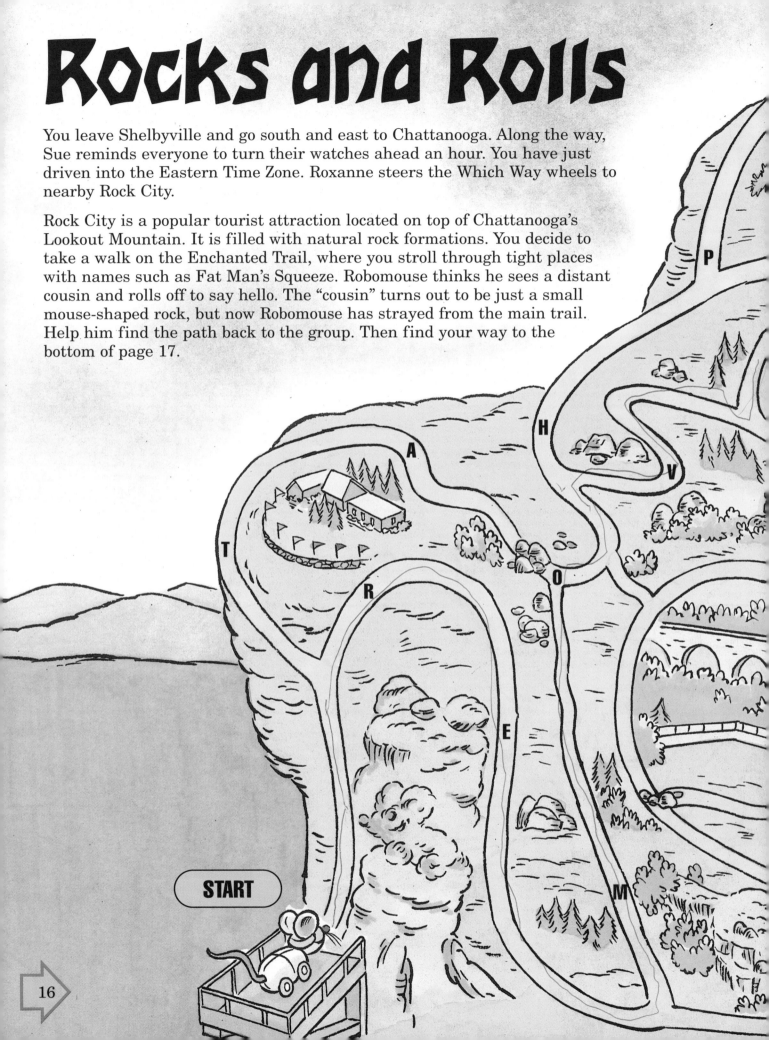

START

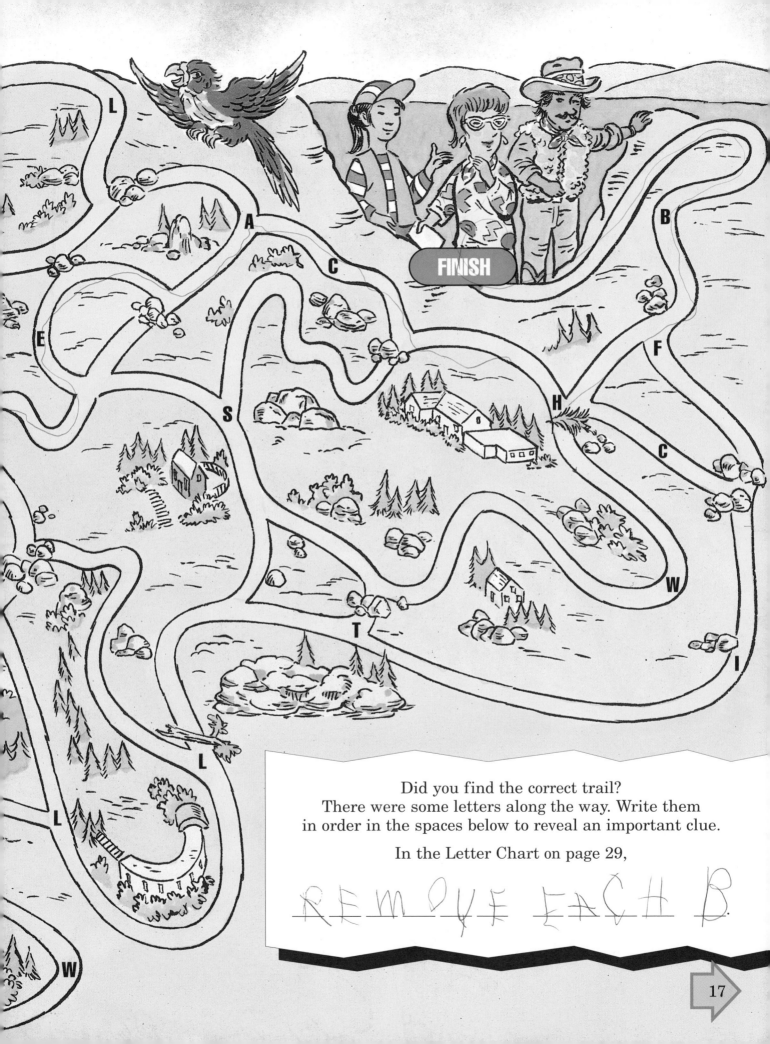

Did you find the correct trail?
There were some letters along the way. Write them
in order in the spaces below to reveal an important clue.

In the Letter Chart on page 29,

R E M O V E   E A C H   B.

Alphabet Accounts

The crew members spend the night in Chattanooga in old railroad cars that have been turned into hotel rooms. Then they hit the road and head northeast. Roxanne rolls up historic Highway 411. Your next stop is the Sequoyah Birthplace Museum in Vonore.

Sequoyah was an important Cherokee leader. He developed an alphabet for the Cherokee language. He is the only person ever known to have single-handedly created an entire alphabet. Thousands of Cherokees learned to read using Sequoyah's symbols.

While examining a display of the alphabet, you see several other visitors. They are also impressed by Sequoyah's work. Now they want to talk about their own accomplishments. Can you figure out which statements are true and which are tall tales? After you do, check the bottom of page 19.

Don't Forget Your Map!
All the answers can be found on your map of Tennessee.

Did you find the false statements?
Count them to reveal your next clue.

If three are false, cross off every C and K.
If four are false, cross off every O and E.
If five are false, cross off every L and G.

Now turn to page 29 and cross off the
correct letters in the chart.

LOST AND FOUND

After saying good-bye to the tour group, the Which Way crew piles into the car. The gang enjoys seeing some beautiful back-country-road scenery as Roxanne drives a few miles west to Craighead Caverns. Tennessee has more than 4,000 known caves. This one is the home of the Lost Sea—the world's largest underground lake.

Roxanne and Sue join a tour group headed for the "Cat Chamber." Bones and footprints of a giant prehistoric jaguar were found in this room of the cave. Robomouse and Squawker want no part of that! They take a glass-bottomed boat tour with Willy, and glide over the $4\frac{1}{2}$-acre Lost Sea within the cave. You board the boat, too. Soon you notice that the lake isn't the only thing lost here. Find the hidden "C" objects. Then sail to the bottom of page 21.

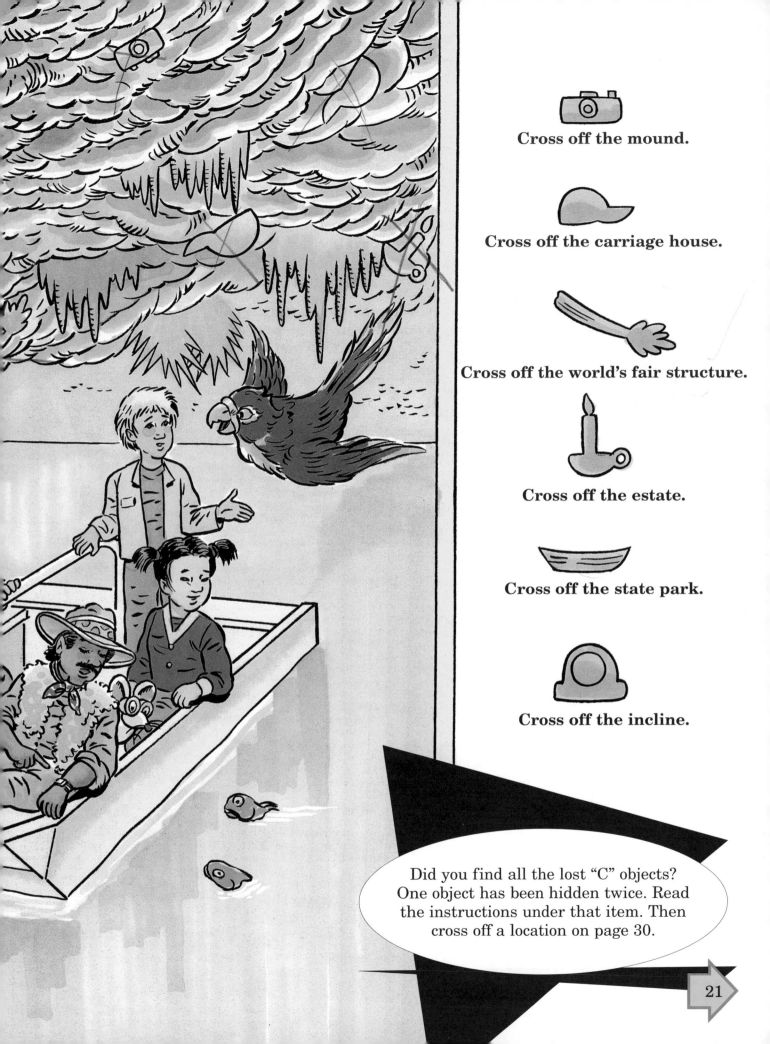

Cross off the mound.

Cross off the carriage house.

Cross off the world's fair structure.

Cross off the estate.

Cross off the state park.

Cross off the incline.

Did you find all the lost "C" objects? One object has been hidden twice. Read the instructions under that item. Then cross off a location on page 30.

Power Trip

The crew returns to the road. Roxanne drives a short distance north to Oak Ridge. Sue wants to see the American Museum of Science and Energy there. Energy has played an important role in Tennessee history. More than fifty dams built in the state by the Tennessee Valley Authority have turned river power into electricity. Also, the city of Oak Ridge was built as part of the "secret" effort to produce atomic weapons during World War II. This museum tells the Oak Ridge story. It also has one of the world's largest exhibits on energy.

Willy checks out an exhibit on static electricity and has a hair-raising experience. You can raise another clue by using your brain power. Fill in the answers to the Tennessee crossword on page 23. Then charge to the bottom of the page.

ACROSS

4. Border city on Interstate 75
6. "Royal" city on the Virginia border in northeast Tennessee
8. Largest city in the state
10. Major river in north-central Tennessee
11. Tennessee's capital
13. "C" city just northeast of 4 Across

DOWN

1. One of the states bordering Tennessee on the south
2. Lake in the southeast corner of Tennessee whose name has more vowels than consonants
3. City with a presidential name northeast of Memphis near I-40
5. Mountain range that the Great Smokies are part of
7. Spelled-out number of the interstate connecting Nashville and Murfreesboro
9. Host city of the "World's Biggest Fish Fry"
12. Watts Bar, Dale Hollow, and Reelfoot: three major _____

Don't Forget Your Map!
Your map of Tennessee has the answers to all these clues.

Did you fill in all the answers? Some of the squares in the grid are shaded. Write the letters from the shaded squares, in order from top to bottom, in the spaces below.

T O W E R

Now turn to page 30 and eliminate the Tennessee landmark this word describes.

Spinning Yarns

The crew members spend the night camping near historic Cumberland Gap. In the morning, they hit the road early. The next stop is Jonesborough, the oldest town in the state. Jonesborough is the headquarters of the National Storytelling Network and Storytelling Foundation International. Each year, these two groups host the National Storytelling Festival. This three-day event attracts storytellers from all over the world.

The festival isn't going on right now, but some local folk have gathered to tell a few tales. You stop to listen to one about Davy Crockett, one of Tennessee's favorite sons. Squawker loves a good story. He decides to mimic this one. But Squawker wasn't listening carefully enough. Can you spot the differences between the two tales? After you do, head to the bottom of page 25.

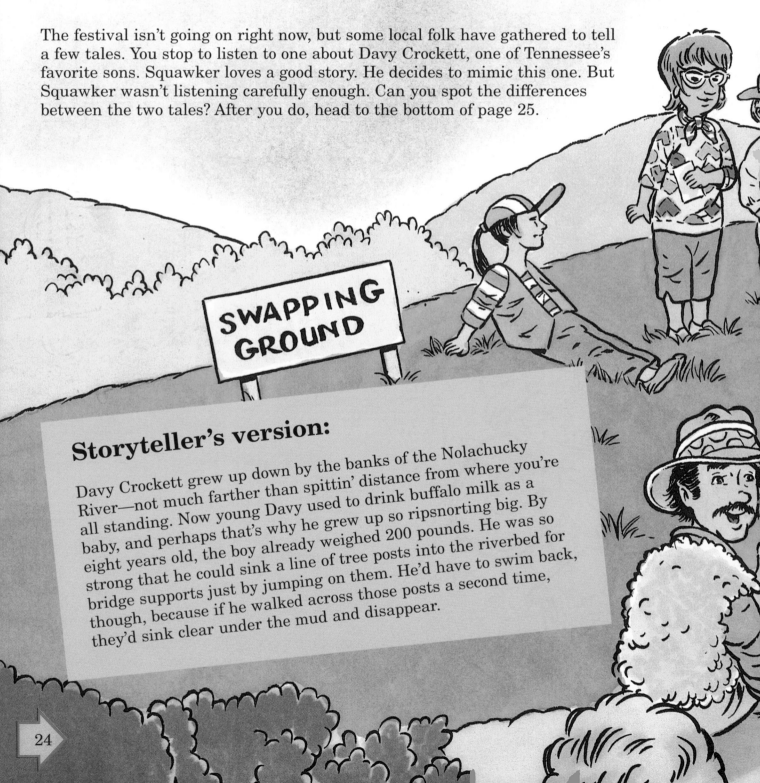

SWAPPING GROUND

Storyteller's version:

Davy Crockett grew up down by the banks of the Nolachucky River—not much farther than spittin' distance from where you're all standing. Now young Davy used to drink buffalo milk as a baby, and perhaps that's why he grew up so ripsnorting big. By eight years old, the boy already weighed 200 pounds. He was so strong that he could sink a line of tree posts into the riverbed for bridge supports just by jumping on them. He'd have to swim back, though, because if he walked across those posts a second time, they'd sink clear under the mud and disappear.

Squawker's version:

Davy Squawkit grew up down by the banks of the Chuckanoly River—not much farther than sittin' distance from where you're all standing. Now young Danny used to drink chocolate milk as a baby, and perhaps that's why he grew up so ripsnorting smart. By seven years old, the boy already weighed 2,000 pounds. He was so strong that he could sink a line of goal posts into the bunk bed for bridge supports just by pecking on them. He'd have to fly back, though, because if he walked across those ghosts a second time, they'd sink clear under the mud and reappear.

To tell the story of how you found another clue, count the number of differences between the storyteller's tale and Squawker's version.

If there are 12 differences, cross off Graceland and the carriage house.

If there are 14 differences, cross off Saul's Mound and the railway.

If there are 16 differences, cross off the Sunsphere and the park.

Now turn to page 30 and use this clue.

On Top of Ol' Smoky

Your last stop in Tennessee is the gorgeous Great Smoky Mountains National Park. The crew decides to end this journey on a high note. Willy leads everyone on a rugged hike to the top of a rocky mountain known as the Chimney Tops. The Chimney Tops are two rock spires rising 4,755 feet in elevation. From the top, you can see stunning views of many other mountain peaks in the park. While everyone relaxes and enjoys the fresh mountain air, you have one more hill to climb.

Read the clues on page 27 and write the answers in the spaces. But be careful! Each of the answers contains only letters found in the words *Great Smoky Mountains*. When you've finished, follow the trail down to the bottom of the page.

1. A compass direction ___E A S T___

2. A toy that flies ___K I T E___

3. A citrus fruit or juice ___O R A N G E___

4. Opposite of weak ___S T R O N G___

5. Small relative of a gorilla ___M O N K E Y___

6. Marries the bride ___G R O O M___

7. Rises from a hot teakettle ___S T E A M___

8. Opposite of difficult ___E A S Y___

9. Big animal with antlers ___M O O S E___

10. Has an engine and a caboose ___T R A I N___

11. Surrounds a castle ___M O A T___

12. Fifty of these in our country ___S T A T E'S___

13. Trick or _____? ___T R E A T___

Did you fill in all the answers?
Some of the letters are circled. Write those
letters in order in the spaces below.

Turn to page 30 and cross off the

___S I N G E R'S___

___E S T A T E.___

Who?

Which famous Tennessean is going into the Which Way Hall of Fame? To find out, you need to solve the puzzles on pages 2 through 11. Each puzzle will help you cross one candidate off the list. When there is only one person left, he or she is the hall-of-famer!

Andrew Jackson
War hero, nicknamed "Old Hickory," who served as the seventh president of the United States

W. C. Handy
Bandleader, composer, and cornet player who is called the "Father of the Blues"

Alex Haley
Pulitzer Prize-winning author who wrote *Roots: The Saga of an American Family*

Cordell Hull
American statesman whose work in founding the United Nations earned him the Nobel Peace Prize

Ida Wells
Journalist, publisher, and one of the nation's first civil-rights workers

Minnie Pearl
Comedienne, actress, and star of the Grand Ole Opry

The person going into the Hall of Fame is: ➡ W. C. Handy

28

What?

One thing from the Volunteer State has been selected for the Which Way Museum. To find out what it is, solve the puzzles on pages 12 through 19. Each puzzle will tell you about some letters to cross off in the Letter Chart. To help you keep track, write the letters on the line next to the page numbers.

Cross off these letters:

Pages 12-13: _U_   Pages 14-15: _remove all vowels in row 4_

Pages 16-17: _B_   Pages 18-19: _L_ and _G_

Now cross off the letters. Write the remaining letters from left to right and from top to bottom in the spaces in the box at the bottom of the page.

LETTER CHART

The item that will go into the Which Way Museum is:

Davy Crocketts
coonskin cap

Where?

One place in Tennessee is to be featured in the Which Way Supermax Movie. To find out where the filming will be, solve the puzzles on pages 20 through 27. Each puzzle will help you eliminate one or more of the famous places below. When you finish, the one place that remains is your answer.

The Sunsphere
A 300-foot-tall tower built for the Tennessee pavilion at the 1982 World's Fair in Knoxville

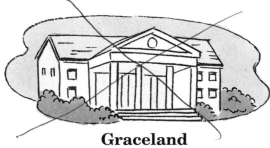

Graceland
Former estate of singer Elvis Presley and one of the most-visited private homes in the country

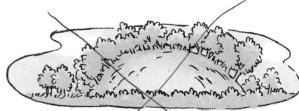

Saul's Mound
Native American mound near Pinson thought to be the second-highest earthen mound in the United States

Fall Creek Falls State Park
Lush park filled with gorges, cliffs, and the highest waterfall in the eastern U.S.

Lookout Mountain Incline Railway
The world's steepest passenger incline railway, located in Chattanooga

Belle Meade Carriage House
Restored building and carriage collection, part of an 1850s plantation

The famous place is:

Fall Creek Falls State Park

All the answers for your
Which Way adventure
are on the next two
pages. Do not go

unless you need help
with a puzzle. If you
don't need help,

before you look at
the answers.

You can use the rest of
this page to work out
your puzzles. If you need
a little extra space,

your pencil here. After
you're done, make a

back to the page you
were working on.

ANSWERS

Pages 2-3: **Memphis Meeting**

The code words tell you to CROSS OUT THE PERSON WHO WROTE *ROOTS*. This eliminates Alex Haley on page 28.

Pages 4-5: **King Clones**

The letters spell OLD HICKORY. Cross off Andrew Jackson on page 28.

Pages 6-7: **The Reel Deal**

The leftover letters spell THE WINNER OF A NOBEL PEACE PRIZE. Cross off Cordell Hull on page 28.

Pages 8-9: **Hello, Shiloh**

1. **o** 2. **p** 3. **r** 4. **y** 5. **s** 6. **t** 7. **a** 8. **r**
The circled letters spell OPRY STAR. Cross off Minnie Pearl on page 28.

Pages 10-11: **A Night at the Opry**

Roxanne's seat is next to the man in the cowboy hat. On page 28, eliminate the civil-rights worker, Ida Wells.

Pages 12-13: **Parthenon Picnic**

1. C H E R O K E E N A T I O N A L F O R E S T
   (1 under O, 2 under F)
2. R O C K R I S I N G T O A P O I N T
   (3 under T, 4 under P)
3. N A S H V I L L E
   (5 under N, 6 under H)
4. A N A T U R E P R E S E R V E
   (7 under A, 8 under T, 9 under R)
5. T H E C I V I L W A R
   (10 under T, 11 under C)
6. N I N E M I L L I O N
   (12 under I, 13 under L)

The message tells you to CROSS OFF EACH U IN THE LETTER CHART. Do this on page 29.

Pages 14-15: **Horsing Around**

The message tells you to

REMOVE ALL VOWELS IN ROW FOUR

Follow the instructions on page 29.

Pages 16-17: **Rocks and Rolls**

The letters along the correct path spell REMOVE EACH B. Do this on page 29.

Pages 18-19: **Alphabet Accounts**

The statement about the world's fair is the only one that doesn't contain a piece of false information. Since five statements are false, cross off every L and G in the letter chart on page 29.